Table of Contents

Introduction

The Occupy movement has brought attention to the great disparity of wealth within the United States; however there has been no clear plan on how to remedy this situation. It is not the intent of anyone to make the rich poor and the poor rich. What is needed is a system that makes it fairer for everyone. The purpose of this book is to present a plan on how to do this.

The country is an economic crisis, how do I know this: all anyone has to do is watch the news and you will see at least one politician, republican, democrat or independent laying the blame on the other party. I don't believe it is any single parties fault, but that they must all take responsibility.

We have all heard about *stimulus packages, corporate tax incentives and tax cuts for the rich,* until it's coming out our ears. Now with an election year coming up, we will hear even more about them. Every politician will be on his soap box with his or her plan, and we can rest assured that each plan will allow the rich to get richer and the poor to get poorer.

Currently President Obama is talking about revising the tax code; well I get nervous when people who make more than a million dollars a year start talking about tax reform. It always seems that the main focus always is on giving the rich tax breaks. Later in this book I will talk about tax reform from a person who has never made over $ 100,000 a year.

Now let's face it the current plans aren't working, and it's time to try something new. Let's look at a plan that does not call itself a *stimulus package,* does not include *corporate tax incentives,* and definitely does not call for more *tax cuts for the rich.*

I do not claim to be a scholar, nor have I studied economics. I am just an individual who has plenty of time on his hands to think and sort through things.

I recall a fable that goes something like this:

An emperor wanted a new set of clothes, not just any old outfit but one that would befit someone of his station. He had his chief advisor to find him the best tailors. The chief advisor searched far a wide until he came upon three men who claimed to be the best tailors in all the land. They claimed that they could tailor a suit for the king that would not only befit one of his station. But would be of such magnificence that only those who were worthy of their position in life would be able to see it. Therefore the emperor would only have the best people in positions of power.

The advisor brought these tailors back to the emperor who was so impressed that he had the tailors begin immediately. The emperor let it be known that these tailors had his full support and that they had been instructed to report to him all those that could not see the clothes as ones that unfit to hold their positions and that they would be immediately banished from the lands.

So the tailors ordered gold and silver that they said they would spin into thread, emeralds and diamonds that would be used like sequins. The tailors locked themselves in the room provided and had a dummy made the same size as the emperor. Anytime anyone ventured into the room the tailors would proudly show off the naked dummy and remark how the emperor was very impressed and how he must be such a great emperor.

Eventually the day came when the emperor was to unveil his new clothes to the whole kingdom. All the people know knew that anyone who was unable to see the clothes was unworthy of their position and would be banished for life.

When the emperor came out of the tailor's room completely naked and all his advisors proclaimed what a wonderful suit of clothes he was wearing, the emperor who could not see the clothes continued on as if he was actually wearing clothes. After all, the emperor couldn't admit he was unable to see any clothes.

It was such an occasion that everyone was on the street waiting to see the emperor's new clothing as it had been reported about the magnificence of the outfit. As the emperor past the people he could hear all of them praising the new clothes as the most beautiful outfit that they had ever seen.

Finally the emperor passed a little boy, the little boy tugged at his mother's dress and said loud enough for all to hear, "Momma, look the emperor is naked." There was a loud gasp from the crowd and then they all realized who had said it, and realized how could a little boy not be worthy of being a little boy. The emperor was in fact naked and the tailor's had conned everyone.

Watching the news and listening to all the politicians talking about their plans to revive the economy, all I can think of is that fable.

The point of this book is not to make the rich poor and the poor rich. The point is to make it so those who are not making megabucks will be able to provide for their families without having to make choices between medicine and food.

Chapter 1

Tax Reform

The Myth

A myth that is very popular in Washington today is that if rich people pay taxes there won't be any money to invest in jobs. I will paraphrase something I heard on the news today:

We can't tax the rich because if we do jobs won't be created.

Let's look at the how that doesn't pass the "look the emperor is naked test."

As an example we give someone who makes $ 10,000,000 a year in gross income a 10 % tax break (assume is tax rate is 32%) that's a break of $ 320,000. According to current Washingtonian thinking this $ 320,000 tax cut will create jobs. Think about that, this is only one person saving $ 320,000; let's say they use that money to buy a Porsche. By giving that tax break you have increased auto sales by one car. Unfortunately there are not enough people making $ 10,000,000 a year to make that great a difference.

Now, let us think about a family of 4 making $ 100,000 or less a year. If they had a tax break (or as you will see later pay no taxes at all) and they use that money to purchase buy a new car. Since there are a lot more families making $ 100,000 or less a year you have just created considerably more buying power then if you give a few a tax break.

Now to me it makes much more sense, that if you sell many less costly items. You will create more jobs than by selling fewer higher priced items.

So if by giving the rich tax breaks we are creating jobs, then why aren't don't we have enough jobs instead of the high unemployment that we are experiencing, after all we have been giving the rich tax breaks ever since Gorge W. Bush was president.

Remember Leona Helmsley and what she said to her maid, it went something like this: "Only the poor pay taxes". Its time to change that!

How much does it cost to Live?

How much money does a family of four needs to live comfortably. Below I have outlined a budget for a family of four. It is an average and I am sure that some people pay less and some people pay more, but I believe it is a fair representation:

Item	Monthly	Yearly	
Housing	$ 2,500.00	$ 30,000.00	Includes: Mortgage, Property Taxes, Insurance, Utilities, Heating
Transportation	$ 1,200.00	$ 14,400.00	Includes: Car Payment, Insurance, Gas
Food	$ 1,000.00	$ 12,000.00	
Medical	$ 500.00	$ 6,000.00	Insurance and Out Pocket expenses
Clothing	$ 500.00	$ 6,000.00	
Total	$ 5,700.00	$ 68,400.00	

Is it broken?

Let's face it the tax system in this country is broken. It is too complicated and only benefits Tax Lawyers, politicians and lobbyist.

Currently it is accepted practice to cheat on your taxes, manipulate the system to reduce your taxes. Just recently a prominent Senator bought a seven million dollar yacht. He promptly registered this yacht in a different state (then his home state) to avoid paying $ 350,000 in taxes. Now I would think that if you can afford a seven million dollar yacht, you should be able to pay the $ 350,000 in taxes, if you can't maybe you should downsize to a six million dollar yacht. I really don't think you would be sacrificing too many luxuries.

So the first step we need to take is to change the countries culture to one that does not venerate tax cheats.

When looking at the tax charts below you shouldn't concern yourself with the amount of tax owed, but what would the tax payer(s) have as after (federal) tax money to live on. Let's take a person, whose gross income is $ 174,999.00, that individual would pay $ 4,375.00 in taxes, so his or hers available money after (federal) tax would be $ 170,624.00. That I believe would be an amount of money that a person could live on. Under the current tax system their tax liability would be $ 40,951.00.

So I propose the following:

Everyone's first $ 50,000 is tax free. This would alleviate the need for Schedule A, the place that most people fudge their tax returns. It would also bring about some fairness in the Tax System. So the tax tables would look something like this (the amounts indicated are based on simple tax prep, no deductions):

Yearly Gross Income $ 0.00 to $ 49,999.00

Currently Pay

Single	$ 0.00 to	$ 5,938.00
After Tax Income	$ 0.00 to	$ 44,061.00
Single w/child(ren)[1]	$ 0.00 to	$ 1,596.00
After Tax Income	$ 0.00 to	$ 48,403.00
Married Filing Jointly	$ 0.00 to	$ 3,054.00
After Tax Income	$ 0.00 to	$ 46,945.00
Married Filing Jointly w/child(ren)[2]	$ 0.00 to	$ 41.00 refund[3]
After Tax Income	$ 0.00 to	$ 50,041.00

Under New Plan

Single	$ 0.00 to	$ 0.00
After Tax Income	$ 0.00 to	$ 49,999.00
Single w/ child(ren)	$ 0.00 to	$ 0.00
After Tax Income	$ 0.00 to	$ 49,999.00
Married Filing Jointly	$ 0.00 to	$ 0.00
After Tax Income	$ 0.00 to	$ 49,999.00
Married Filing Jointly w/child(ren)	$ 0.00 to	$ 0.00
After Tax Income	$ 0.00 to	$ 49,999.00

[1] This person would currently file as head of household. Currently owe figures are based on two children.

[2] Currently owe figures are based on 2two children.

[3] Because of certain Tax Credits a Married Couple with 2 Children would receive a $ 41.00 refund.

Yearly Gross Income $ 50,000.00 to $ 74,999.00

Currently Pay

Single	$ 5,950.00 to	$ 12,188.00
After Tax Income	$ 44,050.00 to	$ 62,811.00
Single w/ child(ren)	$ 1,604.00 to	$ 6,354.00
After Tax Income	$ 48,396.00 to	$ 68,645.00
Married Filing Jointly	$ 3,061.00 to	$ 6,811.00
After Tax Income	$ 46,939.00 to	$ 68,189.00
Married Filing Jointly w/ child(ren)	$ 34.00 refund[4] to	$ 3,709.00
After Tax Income	$ 50,034.00 to	$ 71,290.00

Under New Plan

Single	$ 0.00 to	$ 1,250.00
After Tax Income	$ 50,000.00 to	$ 73,749.00

Rate 5 % for any income over $ 50,000.00

Single w/ child(ren)	$ 0.00 to	$ 0.00
After Tax Income	$ 50,000.00 to	$ 74,999.00
Married Filing Jointly	$ 0.00 to	$ 0.00
After Tax Income	$ 50,000.00 to	$ 74,999.00
Married Filing Jointly w/child(ren)	$ 0.00 to	$ 0.00
After Tax Income	$ 50,000.00 to	$ 74,999.00

---

[4] Because of certain Tax Credits a Married Couple with 2 Children would receive a $ 34.00 refund. Please note that by earning $ 1.00 more they are losing $ 7.00 of their refund.

Yearly Gross Income $ 75,000.00 to $ 99,999.00

Currently Pay

Single	$ 12,200.00 to	$ 19,084.00
After Tax Income	$ 62,800.00 to	$ 80,915.00
Single w/child(ren)	$ 6,366.00 to	$ 14,254.00
After Tax Income	$ 68,634.00 to	$ 85,733.00
Married Filing Jointly	$ 6,811.00 to	$ 11,881.00
After Tax Income	$ 68,189.00 to	$ 88,118.00
Married Filing Jointly w/child(ren)	$ 3,716.00 to	$ 8,056.00
After Tax Income	$ 71,284.00 to	$ 91,930.00

Under New Plan

Single	$ 1,250.00 to	$ 3,750.00
After Tax Income	$ 73,750.00 to	$ 96,250.00

Rate 10 % for any income over $ 75,000.00 plus any previous amount

Single w/child(ren)	$ 0.00 to	$ 0.00
After Tax Income	$ 75,000.00 to	$ 99,999.00
Married Filing Jointly	$ 0.00 to	$ 0.00
After Tax Income	$ 75,000.00 to	$ 99,999.00
Married Filing Jointly w/child(ren)	$ 0.00 to	$ 0.00
After Tax Income	$ 75,000.00 to	$ 99,999.00

Yearly Gross Income $ 100,000.00 to $ 124,999.00

Currently Pay

Single	$ 19,098.00 to	$ 26,091.00
After Tax Income	$ 80,902.00 to	$ 98,909.00
Single w/child(ren)	$ 14,266.00 to	$ 21,260.00
After Tax Income	$ 85,734.00 to	$ 103,740.00
Married Filing Jointly	$ 11,894.00 to	$ 18,137.00
After Tax Income	$ 88,106.00 to	$ 106,862.00
Married Filing Jointly w/child(ren)	$ 8,069.00 to	$ 15,056.00
After Tax Income	$ 91,931.00 to	$ 109,943.00

Under New Plan

Single	$ 3,750.00 to	$ 7,500.00
After Tax Income	$ 96,250.00 to	$ 117,499.00

Rate 15 % for any income over $ 100,000.00 plus any previous amount

Single w/child(ren)	$ 0.00 to	$ 2,500.00
After Tax Income	$ 100,000.00 to	$ 122,499.00

Rate 10 % for any income over $ 100,000.00

Married Filing Jointly	$ 0.00 to	$ 2,500.00
After Tax Income	$ 100,000.00 to	$ 122,499.00

Rate 10 % for any income over $ 100,000.00

Married Filing Jointly w/child(ren)	$ 0.00 to	$ 2,500.00
After Tax Income	$ 100,000.00 to	$ 122,499.00

Rate 10 % for any income over $ 100,000.00

Yearly Gross Income $ 125,000.00 to $ 149,999.00

Currently Pay

Single	$ 26,091.00	to	$ 33,091.00
After Tax Income	$ 98,909.00	to	$ 116,908.00
Single w/child(ren)	$ 21,260.00	to	$ 29,100.00
After Tax Income	$ 103,740.00	to	$ 120,899.00
Married Filing Jointly	$ 18,138.00	to	$ 24,387.00
After Tax Income	$ 106,862.00	to	$ 125,612.00
Married Filing Jointly w/child(ren)	$ 15,069.00	to	$ 22,562.00
After Tax Income	$ 109,931.00	to	$ 127,437.00

Under New Plan

Single	$ 7,500.00	to	$ 12,500.00
After Tax Income	$ 117,500.00	to	$ 137,499.00

Rate 20 % for any income over $ 125,000.00 plus any previous amount

Single w/child(ren)	$ 2,500.00	to	$ 6,250.00
After Tax Income	$ 122,500.00	to	$ 143,749.00

Rate 15 % for any income over $ 125,000.00 plus any previous amount

Married Filing Jointly	$ 2,500.00	to	$ 6,250.00
After Tax Income	$ 122,500.00	to	$ 143,749.00

Rate 15 % for any income over $ 125,000.00 plus any previous amount

Married Filing Jointly w/child(ren)	$ 2,500.00	to	$ 6,250.00
After Tax Income	$ 122,500.00	to	$ 143,749.00

Rate 15 % for any income over $ 125,000.00 plus any previous amount

Yearly Gross Income $ 150,000.00 to $ 174,999.00

Currently Pay
Single..$ 33,091.00 to $ 40,091.00
    After Tax Income........................$ 116,909.00 to $ 134,909.00
Single w/child(ren)............................$ 29,101.00 to $ 37,225.00
    After Tax Income........................$ 120,899.00 to $ 137,774.00
Married Filing Jointly........................$ 24,388.00 to $ 32,007.00
    After Tax Income........................$ 125,612.00 to $ 142,992.00
Married Filing Jointly w/child(ren)........$ 22,563.00 to $ 29,963.00
    After Tax Income ....$ 127,437.00 to $ 145,036.00

Under New Plan
Single..$ 12,500.00 to $ 18,950.00
    After Tax Income........................$ 137,500.00 to $ 156,049.00
Rate 25 % for any income over $ 150,000.00 plus any previous amount
Single w/child(ren)............................$ 6,250.00 to $ 11,250.00
    After Tax Income........................$ 143,750.00 to $ 163,749.00
Rate 20 % for any income over $ 150,000.00 plus any previous amount
Married Filing Jointly........................$ 6,250.00 to $ 11,250.00
    After Tax Income........................$ 143,750.00 to $ 163,749.00
Rate 20 % for any income over $ 150,000.00 plus any previous amount
Married Filing Jointly w/child(ren)........$ 6,250.00 to $ 11,250.00
    After Tax Income........................$143,750.00 to $ 163,749.00
  Rate 20 % for any income over $ 150,000.00 plus any previous amount

Yearly Gross Income $ 175,000.00 to $ 199,999.00

Currently Pay

Single .... $ 40,091.00 to $ 48,031.00
    After Tax Income .... $ 134,909.00 to $ 151,968.00
Single w/child(ren) .... $ 37,226.00 to $ 45,350.00
    After Tax Income .... $ 137,774.00 to $ 154,649.00
Married Filing Jointly .... $ 32,008.00 to $ 39,007.00
    After Tax Income .... $ 142,992.00 to $ 160,992.00
Married Filing Jointly w/child(ren) .... $ 29,964.00 to $ 36,963.00
    After Tax Income .... $ 145,036.00 to $ 163,036.00

Under New Plan

Single .... $ 18,950.00 to $ 26,400.00
    After Tax Income .... $ 156,050.00 to $ 173,599.00
Rate 30 % for any income over $ 175,000 plus any previous amount
Single w/child(ren) .... $ 11,250.00 to $ 17,500.00
    After Tax Income .... $ 163,750.00 to $ 182,499.00
Rate 25 % for any income over $ 175,000.00 plus any previous amount
Married Filing Jointly .... $ 11,250.00 to $ 17,500.00
    After Tax Income .... $ 163,750.00 to $ 182,499.00
Rate 25 % for any income over $ 175,000.00 plus any previous amount
Married Filing Jointly w/child(ren) .... $ 11,250.00 to $ 17,500.00
    After Tax Income .... $ 163,750.00 to $ 182,499.00
Rate 25 % for any income over $ 175,000.00 plus any previous amount

Yearly Gross Income $ 200,000.00 to $ 249,999.00

Currently Pay

Single	$ 48,031.00 to	$ 64,531.00
After Tax Income	$ 151,969.00 to	$ 185,468.00
Single w/child(ren)	$ 45,351.00 to	$ 62,839.00
After Tax Income	$ 154,649.00 to	$ 187,160.00
Married Filing Jointly	$ 39,008.00 to	$ 54,110.00
After Tax Income	$ 160,992.00 to	$ 195,889.00
Married Filing Jointly w/child(ren)	$ 36,964.00 to	$ 53,214.00
After Tax Income	$ 163,036.00 to	$ 196,785.00

Under New Plan

Single	$ 26,400.00 to	$ 45,150.00
After Tax Income	$ 173,600.00 to	$ 204,849.00

Rate 37.5 % for any income over $ 200,000 plus any previous amount

Single w/child(ren)	$ 17,500.00 to	$ 35,000.00
After Tax Income	$ 182,500.00 to	$ 214,999.00

Rate 35 % for any income over $ 200,000.00 plus any previous amount

Married Filing Jointly	$ 17,500.00 to	$ 35,000.00
After Tax Income	$ 182,500.00 to	$ 214,999.00

Rate 35 % for any income over $ 200,000.00 plus any previous amount

Married Filing Jointly w/child(ren)	$ 17,500.00 to	$ 35,000.00
After Tax Income	$ 182,500.00 to	$ 214,999.00

Rate 35 % for any income over $ 200,000.00 plus any previous amount

Yearly Gross Income $ 250,000.00 to $ 499,999.00

Currently Pay

Single .... $ 64,531.00 to $ 149,371.00
    After Tax Income .... $ 185,469.00 to $ 350,628.00
Single w/child(ren) .... $ 62,839.00 to $ 142,545.00
    After Tax Income .... $ 187,161.00 to $ 357,454.00
Married Filing Jointly .... $ 54,110.00 to $ 138,763.00
    After Tax Income .... $ 195,890.00 to $ 361,236.00
Married Filing Jointly w/child(ren) .... $ 53,214.00 to $ 136,500.00
    After Tax Income .... $ 196,786.00 to $ 363,499.00

Under New Plan

Single .... $ 60,000.00 to $ 160,000.00
    After Tax Income .... $ 190,000.00 to $ 339,999.00
Rate 40 % for any income over $ 100,000.00
Single w/child(ren) .... $ 56,250.00 to $ 150,000.00
    After Tax Income .... $ 193,750.00 to $ 349,999.00
Rate 37.5 % for any income over $ 100,000.00
Married Filing Jointly .... $ 56,250.00 to $ 150,000.00
    After Tax Income .... $ 193,750.00 to $ 349,999.00
Rate 37.5 % for any income over $ 100,000.00
Married Filing Jointly w/child(ren) .... $ 56,250.00 to $ 150,000.00
    After Tax Income .... $ 193,750.00 to $ 349,999.00
Rate 37.5 % for any income over $ 100,000.00

Yearly Gross Income $ 500,000.00 to $ 999,999.00

Currently Pay
Single..$ 149,371.00 to $ 324,371.00
    After Tax Income.....................$ 350,629.00 to $ 675,628.00
Single w/child(ren).............................$ 142,545.00 to $ 317,545.00
    After Tax Income.....................$ 357,455.00 to $ 682,454.00
Married Filing Jointly.........................$ 138,763.00 to $ 313,763.00
    After Tax Income.....................$ 361,237.00 to $ 686,236.00
Married Filing Jointly w/child(ren).........$ 136,500.00 to $ 311,208.00
    After Tax Income......................$ 363,500.00 to $ 688,791.00

Under New Plan
Single..$ 170,000.00 to $ 382,500.00
    After Tax Income.....................$ 330,000.00 to $ 617,999.00
Rate 42.5 % for any income over $ 100,000.00
Single w/child(ren).............................$ 160,000.00 to $ 360,000.00
    After Tax Income.....................$ 340,000.00 to $ 639,999.00
Rate 40 % for any income over $ 100,000.00
Married Filing Jointly.........................$ 160,000.00 to $ 360,000.00
    After Tax Income.....................$ 340,000.00 to $ 639,999.00
Rate 40 % for any income over $ 100,000.00
Married Filing Jointly w/child(ren).........$ 160,000.00 to $ 360,000.00
    After Tax Income.....................$ 340,000.00 to $ 639,999.00
Rate 40 % for any income over $ 100,000.00

Yearly Gross Income $ 1,000,000.00 to $ 4,999,999.00

Currently Pay

Single .... $ 324,371.00 to $ 1,724,371.00
    After Tax Income .... $ 675,629.00 to $ 3,275,628.00
Single w/child(ren) .... $ 317,545.00 to $ 1,717,545.00
    After Tax Income .... $ 682,455.00 to $ 3,282,454.00
Married Filing Jointly .... $ 313,763.00 to $ 1,713,763.00
    After Tax Income .... $ 686,237.00 to $ 3,286,236.00
Married Filing Jointly w/child(ren) .... $ 311,208.00 to $ 1,711,208.00
    After Tax Income .... $ 688,792.00 to $ 3,288,791.00

Under New Plan

Single .... $ 405,000.00 to $ 2,205,000.00
    After Tax Income .... $ 595,000.00 to $ 2,794,999.00
Rate 45 % for any income over $ 100,000.00
Single w/child(ren) .... $ 382,500.00 to $ 2,082,500.00
    After Tax Income .... $ 617,500.00 to $ 2,917,499.00
Rate 42.5 % for any income over $ 100,000.00
Married Filing Jointly .... $ 382,500.00 to $ 2,082,500.00
    After Tax Income .... $ 617,500.00 to $ 2,917,499.00
Rate 42.5 % for any income over $ 100,000.00
Married Filing Jointly w/child(ren) .... $ 382,500.00 to $ 2,082,500.00
    After Tax Income .... $ 617,500.00 to $ 2,917,499.00
Rate 42.5 % for any income over $ 100,000.00

Yearly Gross Income $ 5,000,000.00 to $ 9,999,999.00

Currently Pay
Single .... $ 1,724,371.00 to $ 3,474,371.00
    After Tax Income .... $ 3,275,629.00 to $ 6,525,628.00
Single w/child(ren) .... $ 1,717,545.00 to $ 3,467,545.00
    After Tax Income .... $ 3,282,455.00 to $ 6,532,454.00
Married Filing Jointly .... $ 1,713,763.00 to $ 3,463,763.00
    After Tax Income .... $ 3,286,237.00 to $ 6,536,236.00
Married Filing Jointly w/child(ren) .... $ 1,711,208.00 to $ 3,461,208.00
    After Tax Income .... $ 3,288,792.00 to $ 6,538,791.00

Under New Plan
Single .... $ 2,205,000.00 to $ 4,455,000.00
    After Tax Income .... $ 2,795,000.00 to $ 5,544,999.00
Rate 45 % for any income over $ 100,000.00
Single w/child(ren) .... $ 2,205,000.00 to $ 4,455,000.00
    After Tax Income .... $ 2,795,000.00 to $ 5,544,999.00
Rate 45 % for any income over $ 100,000.00
Married Filing Jointly .... $ 2,205,000.00 to $ 4,455,000.00
    After Tax Income .... $ 2,795,000.00 to $ 5,544,999.00
Rate 45 % for any income over $ 100,000.00
Married Filing Jointly w/child(ren) .... $ 2,205,000.00 to $ 4,455,000.00
    After Tax Income .... $ 2,795,000.00 to $ 5,544,999.00
Rate 45 % for any income over $ 100,000.00

Yearly Gross Income Over $ 10,000,000.00[5]

The tax rate for people earning over $ 10,000,000 would be 45 % of all income.

---

[5] I will not be comparing what a person(s) would currently be paying because as has been demonstrated previously it is less then what is being proposed.

Chapter 2
Business & Corporate Taxes

I just read an article that states that 30 of the biggest corporation did not pay any federal taxes in the last 3 years. Think about that, did you pay any federal taxes in the last 3 years, I did, and even though I am retired I will pay taxes again this year on my retirement income.

It is time to change this!!!

Again it is important to keep things simple and what I am proposing would be simple.

The first $ 100,000.00 of adjusted gross business or corporate profit would be Tax Free. This would give small businesses a chance to survive.

After the first $ 100,000.00 there would be a 1% tax on, what I will call Adjusted Gross Profit. Adjusted Gross Profit would be any income that is earned minus the cost of any material directly used in manufacture of another product.

Let's use the example of car manufacturing. The cost of all material directly used to manufacture the car would be deducted from the Sale Price to come up with an Adjusted Gross Profit. So let's say that the car manufacturer sells a car they have made for $ 16,000.00, the cost of all the items needed to make this car (engine, tires, rims, radio, etc) is $ 10,000.00. The Adjusted Gross Profit on that car would be $ 6,000.00. That would make the car manufacturer libel for $ 60.00 in federal taxes (after the manufacturers first $ 100,000.00).

Businesses that do not manufacture anything, such as Lawyers, Accountants, etc would be taxed on all income. An example a lawyer charges a client $ 20,000.00 to handle a civil lawsuit. The lawyer would have a tax liability of $ 200.00.

The 1% tax would only be on the Adjusted Gross Profit. This would assure that all major corporations would pay at least some degree of taxes.

There would also be taxes on Net Profits. This would allow businesses and corporations to deduct such items and salaries, electricity, transportation, etc. Basically all the normal expenses associated with running a business.

Below is the tax rate schedule for businesses and corporations:

$ 100,000.00 to $ 150,000.00 Net Profit
10% of any amount over $ 100,000.00

$ 150,001.00 to $ 200,000.00 Net Profit
15 % of any amount over $ 150,001.00 plus any previous amount

$ 200,001.00 to $ 300,000.00 Net Profit
20 % of any amount over $ 200,001.00 plus any previous amount

$ 300,001.00 to $ 500,000.00 Net Profit
25 % of any amount over $ 300,001.00 plus any previous amount

$ 500,001.00 to $ 1,000,000.00 Net Profit
30 % of any amount over $ 500,001.00 plus any previous amount

Over $ 1,000,001.00 Net Profit
35 % of any amount over $ 1,000.001.00 plus any previous amount

As you can see the tax rates for businesses and corporations do not go as high as that for individuals. This would allow businesses and corporations to pay their owner(s), in the case of corporations the stock holders more money. This would be an incentive for people to become entrepreneurs and create jobs for others.

As stated earlier the tax system must be simple and easy to understand. I understand fully that there are a lot of details that need to be worked out, and that would be left to the professionals.

Salaries

In today's world it is not unusual to hear of top executives receiving multi-million dollar salaries. While I am sure they deserve proper compensation these salaries are sometimes way over the top, especially when you then hear that the company has posted its multi-billion dollar loses for sixth straight quarter. It just doesn't seem to make sense to me.

Under the simpler Tax system that I am proposing there would be a ten percent surtax on any salary or compensation package valued at over a million dollars. So if a top executive of the corporation has a compensation package (includes salary, stock options, etc) that totals ten million dollars the corporation would incur a surtax of one million dollars.

This might encourage corporations to hire executives that are going to increase profitability.

Bonuses

We have all heard the stories XYZ Corp. posts a twenty-five billion dollar loss. Yet the CEO receives a ten million dollar bonus, does that make sense to anyone.

So under the new tax system there would be four rules regarding bonuses. They are as follows:

Any company, corporation or enterprise that does not show a taxable profit will not be allowed to pay out bonuses.

Bonuses may not exceed the amount of the company, corporation or enterprise's taxable profit.

Bonuses for any individual that total over one million dollars will not be tax deductable.

Bonuses for any individual that total over one million dollars will incur a twenty percent surtax. So if the Chief Executive Officer of XYZ Corporation receives a five million dollar bonus, the corporation would be responsible for one million dollar surtax.

Chapter 3
Other Taxes

Remembering that the country is in a fiscal crisis and we must make some changes to the tax system, there are other taxes that I would propose. This goes against the national trend that has been prevalent over the last couple of decades of no new taxes. But, as can be seen this has not worked. So please bear with me and look at these with an open mind.

National Property Tax

Yes, a National Property Tax! Remember under the tax system that I am proposing everyone's (except those people making megabucks) income tax will be decreasing and they will be having more money available to them.

The tax that I am proposing is much less then what most people pay now in property tax. It would be .001 % of the accesses value. An example: Let's say your house is currently appraised for $ 250,000.00. Your national property tax would be $ 250.00; even under today's tax system I believe that amount would be doable.

I had recently heard on the news that a prominent sports figure was building a fifty-five million dollar "bachelor pad". So this person's national property tax would be fifty-five thousand, while that looks like a lot, if he is building a fifty-five million dollar house and can't afford another fifty-five thousand perhaps he should down size to thirty million dollar home and the twenty-five million dollars he saves could be banked and just the interest would pay his national property tax. Even at only thirty million dollars this home would properly be livable and have many amenities that most people do not have.

National Sales Tax

I propose a five percent national sales tax on any item with a value of one hundred thousand dollars or more. This would not be a burden on most people. If you recall in the beginning of this book I told the story of the senator who bought a seven million dollar yacht but registered it in a different state to avoid paying a five percent tax on it. Well I go back to, if he couldn't afford the extra three hundred fifty thousand dollar maybe he should have downsized to a six million dollar yacht.

So the tax would work like this, the senator (same one as mentioned above) buys his yacht, he would be liable for a five percent national sales tax in this case three hundred fifty thousand dollars. If for some reason he could not afford the extra three hundred fifty thousand he could always downsize to a six million dollar yacht and pay the three hundred thousand dollar sales tax out of the million dollars he saved. I really don't believe that he would be that disappointed with a six million dollar yacht.

Trust Fund Surtax

There are two points that I have made previously in this book. One was that it is not my intent to make the rich poor and the poor rich: and the other point is that the country is in financial crisis. It is with this in mind that I propose a onetime surtax on any trust fund that has a value of one hundred million dollars or more. This surtax would be a ten percent tax. It would go into effect and have a very short life, probably no more than five years.

Again we need to look at what that would mean to the individual(s) whose trust fund would be affected. Let just say that a person has a trust fund valued at one hundred million dollars, (s)he earns five percent on this trust fund. That would give them an annual income of five million dollars. If we figure in the surtax this will reduce the annual income to four million five hundred thousand. Again I believe that the individual would be able to live rather comfortably on that amount.

Miscellaneous Taxes

Tobacco Taxes

I have spent most of my life working in a prison and while there I learned that where ever there is a demand, there will be someone who will be a supplier. The system where I worked banned tobacco products several years ago. That changed numerous dynamic within the walls. There was a shift in the trafficking of contraband, the major players stopped trying to get drugs in and went to getting tobacco in. Hand rolled cigarettes would sell for $ 5.00 a piece and packs of cigarettes would sell for $ 50.00 each. This showed me the addictive power of tobacco, and the willingness of people to pay any price to feed that addiction.

So if the government doubled the tax on tobacco it would not lessen the demand any, and the tax could be used to fund medical care for those who suffer from the ill effects of years of smoking.

Alcohol Taxes

Doubling the taxes on alcohol would not affect the consumption of this product, but could provide substantial additional revenue. We need to remember that we need to reduce the deficit and balance the budget.

Gambling (Lottery)

Change the way taxes are assessed on the lottery. Instead of taxing a person's winnings, put a five cent tax on each dollar spent. While this may seem radical it only makes sense.

Casino gambling winnings would be considered income and would be taxed like any other income.

Legalize Marijuana and Tax it

This is probably the most radical part of this plan. Let us be honest, marijuana is here to stay and no matter how many laws are passed outlawing it, it will always be here. Now the argument will be made that this will send us down the slippery slope of legalizing all drug use. I don't believe it will. It would be Taxed on the same basis as tobacco.

Chapter 4
Economic Stimulus

How do we get the economy working again? Well I have a plan for that. I have heard many news stories about the woes of different industries (auto, banking and housing) and the government's plans to jump start the economy. The government first bailed out the auto industry and this was supposed to get the economy going. Then it was the banking industry, and again this was supposed to get things going. Neither of these plans worked.

So why don't we try bailing out the people. With the tax reform plan outlined previously it is obvious that people will have more money to spend, but with the burden of previous debt holding people back I think it will take more than this to get the economy going. Here is my plan:

Everyone who earns less than one hundred thousand dollars a year would be eligible for a one time loan from the government of two hundred fifty thousand dollars. This would allow everyone a chance to catch-up and people would be able to make payment through payroll deductions, just like taxes. The loans would be issued with an interest rate of 1.5 %, or a payment schedule as follows (remember this will done through payroll deductions just like taxes are now.)

Weekly Payments	$ 199.03
Bi-Weekly	$ 398.11
Monthly	$ 862.80

People would still have to use their property for collateral just like they do now. Once the item is sold the government would receive whatever is owed, just like now.

So this is how it will work, a family owns two cars, a mortgage, a home equity loan, student loans and has credit card debt. They have loans out on these items:

Reason for loan	Balance	Monthly Payment
The car loans have a balance of	$ 32,000.00	$ 850.00
The mortgage	$ 100,000.00	$ 1,000.00
The home equity loan	$ 45,000.00	$ 500.00
Student Loans	$ 35,000.00	$ 350.00
Credit Cards	$ 20,000.00	$ 850.00
Total Debt	$ 232,000.00	$ 3,450.00

So should this family take advantage of the program then their monthly payment would be:

	Payment	Savings
Weekly	$ 184.70	$ 2,711.20
Bi-Weekly	$ 369.45	$ 2,711.10
Monthly	$ 800.68	$ 2,649.32

As this example shows this family would have an extra $ 2,649.32 per month. While it would be nice to think that this would then go into saving, it will probably be used to improve their lives allowing them to take that vacation they always wanted.

This plan would also bail out the banking industry, and with the extra people would probably be more willing to purchase a new car, again helping the auto industry.

Collecting these debts would not be a problem since the government has the ultimate debt collecting capabilities already in place with the IRS.

Chapter 5
How can we get this plan implemented?

Obviously this plan will not be implemented simple because you read this book and think it is a good idea. You must take action, what type of action you ask? Let your elected officials know that you support this plan.

Send them a copy of this book with a letter telling them you support this plan and ask for a written response (see Appendix A for a list of websites that will provide you with your Senators and Representatives addresses). Tell them that their support of this plan is vital to any plans they may have to stay in office, because if they do not support this plan you will find someone who does and that person will get your vote. Remember all politicians want to stay in office it there base of power. Just don't send it to your federal representatives, send it to your local officials as well, by sheer volume they should get the message. Remember send a hard copy rather than an e-mail or electronic copy, it is just too easy to hit the delete button and ignore electronic messages.

Don't stop at your representatives, sent copies to the head of the republican and democratic parties. Send it to local and national news media also, the more people who get the message the better..

We, the people, have the power in this country to change things; we just need to make our voices heard. If our current elected officials won't make changes then we should change them. Find people in your area who are willing to fight for this and vote them into office.

Hard copies of this book should be available on Amazon.com and other retailers by November 25.

Appendix A

Below is a list of your websites that will give you contact information for your Senators and Congressman and how to contact them.

http://www.contactingthecongress.org

This website provides the addresses for the Washington Offices and all local offices along with phone number and FAX number.

http://www.usa.gov/Contact/Elected.shtml

This website provides the addresses for the Washington Offices and all local offices along with phone number and FAX number.

http://www.house.gov

Provide links to members of the House of Representatives websites.

Appendix B

Sample letters to your elected officials, these letters should be hand written and sent with a copy of this book. Politicians pay attention when faced with considerable public pressure.

Other notable people who you may want to send these too would be, heads of each political party, network news anchors, local news anchors, local newspapers and anyone else who you think would be someone who would get the word out.

To your Congressperson or Senator

To The Honorable (Name),

I am sending you a copy of the book *"The Occupy Wall Street Guide to Tax Reform and Economic Recovery"*. I have reviewed the plans contained in this book and agree that they should be implemented as soon as practical.

You should also know that your support or lack thereof will be something that I will consider when deciding whom to vote for in the next election. Those who support this plan will also receive my support and my vote.

As you may have noticed this movement has major support amongst many American, and you and your colleague should take notice.

I ask you to please review the book and respond to this letter with your thoughts.

Thanking you advance for your time.

Sincerely,

Your Signature

Print your name and address.

To your local elected officials:

(Elected Official Name and Title),

I am sending you a copy of the book *"The Occupy Wall Street Guide to Tax Reform and Economic Recovery"*. I have reviewed the plans contained in this book and agree that they should be implemented as soon as practical.

I am requesting that you contact our congressional delegation in Washington and inform them of the people of (your state) desire to have this plan implemented as soon as practical.

You should also know that your support or lack thereof will be something that I will consider when deciding whom to vote for in the next election. Those who support this plan will also receive my support and my vote.

I ask you to please review the book and respond to this letter with your thoughts.

Thanking you advance for your time.

Sincerely,

Your Signature

Print your name and address